THE ULTIMATE GL

PROPERTY INVESTMENT

HOW TO MAKE BIG MONEY

Powerful Techniques anyone can use to replace their salary and escape the rat race quickly.

You have incredible untapped potential residing within yourself.

This book shows you how to invest even if you have none of your own money to invest.

Sumit Gupta

AssocRICS B.Com (Hons) PGDBA (FINANCE) MBA (INTERNATIONAL BUSINESS)

An entrepreneur, Author, Property Investor & Mentor

Presented by:

Global Property Consulting

Disclaimer

The information in this book is for education purpose only. The contents do not constitute financial and legal advice in any way. You should seek independent professional advice before making any investment.

This book is available online, kindle, our centres and in Book stores.

Table of Contents

Acknowledgements 4

Prologue 9

Chapter 1: Introduction 15

Chapter 2: Why to invest in property 32

Chapter 3: Make your power team and gather your personal resources

.... 44

Chapter 4: Analysing the market and How to find the deals 51

Chapter 5: Negotiation Techniques that Create Win-Win Situation 59

Chapter 6: LEARN LEVERAGING - You do not have to do everything

yourself 73

Chapter 7: Eleven Successful Property investment STRATEGIES 76

Chapter 8: The best investment 96

About Sumit Gupta 109

ACKNOWLEDGEMENTS

I would not be the person I am today without the love, support and influence of many people.

To my beautiful wife Poonam, you are my soul mate and support. I am so grateful for the tireless work and great caring you give to me and our kids.

To my children Yash and Arnav, you're all unique and amazingly great. I am proud to be your Dad. You bring joy and purpose to my life. Thank you for being my reason to strive and be alive.

To My mom and dad, for giving any positive and negative inspiration in my life.

To Andy, you awakened the giant within me, and gave me the push I needed to complete my long awaited book. Without you, this book might have taken another few years for me to complete.

To my Guru, SRI SRI Ravi Shankar who has helped me throughout my life to be a better human being. Your taught meditation techniques made me a better person, helped me maintain the centeredness in any difficult situation and keeping calm mind. These techniques really help me in anything I do in my life.

To Emily and Amit Garg, who assisted me in editing this book.

To Yash, who inspired me always to complete this book.

SEVEN UNIVERSAL TRUTHS

Truth No. 1

Everything and I mean everything you want to achieve begins with a thought. So allow yourself the time and space to daydream, visualize, and use your imagination to craft the most amazing scenarios of what you want your life to be.

Truth No. 2

No matter where you are in your life, you will always be able to come up with an excuse to wait.

Truth No. 3

Everything that has happened in your life, whether good or bad, has happened for a reason. Your experience have gifted you a unique empathy with people who face what you faced.

Truth No. 4

The knowledge, know-how and experience you have acquired to date are valuable asset. The most important investment you can make is in yourself.

Truth No. 5

The world has changed. You no longer need to be skilled & experienced and allowing an employer to capitalise on that knowledge and wisdom whole you get paid fraction of what they are making our of you.

Truth No. 6

You can reach thousands if no millions of people using social media and internet outreach.

Truth No. 7

If you want different results, you have to do things differently.

If any of these truths have resonated with you and if you have not done so already, please invest in this book and I will reveal to you the strategies for property investment step by steps.

Sumit Gupta

But before we begin our journey together, there is something I think you ought to know.....

PROLOGUE

Have you ever had dreamt to achieve something really BIG in your life? Yes, even I did?

If you were with me around November 2004 in India city called Mumbai, you would have found me very slowly entering through a door. I am seeing him sitting on a sofa watching TV, a dark place and light flickering. He is around 5.10 feet tall with white hair. His piercing eyes are looking like typical father. He asked me where were you until this late night.

I was like what do I say, how will he react. He says "Is this a time to come home, its 11pm" I said "Dad, I attended a seminar where I met a guy who was teaching dream big, become rich, learn and earn in UK"

Dad "that is not for you son. They all are crook".

I "No, this sounds so appealing; I do not want to do a job like this for rest of my life".

Dad "what's wrong with you, you have a secure job working for Standard chartered bank"

I "Dad, secure job? Job is not my future. I want to do something bigger and better in my life. See I read this book *Rich Dad Poor Dad*, Robert teaches about investment. My salary is not enough to save enough, how do I invest?" "Dad I've decided to go to UK to do further study and work, I will earn lots of money and do something better with my life"

Dad "Son, do not mess up with your secure job & future and anyways I do not have money to give you. These people show big dream to sell their products". I said "NN...No dad.....He said "just shut up... end of discussion".

I am like, I have decided so I will have to do it somehow. Just to cut my story short, after few months of great struggle & lots of efforts, lots of argument with family, I managed to turn this impossible looking task possible. I took out all my savings from the bank, encashed my PF funds, sold whatever I could and still could get only 20% of my UK study fee. To overcome this hurdle I then borrowed the rest from the bank, resigned my bank job and came to UK; effectively with lots of debts and enchased almost everything I had in India and left my so-called secured job.

After paying all my course fee and flight tickets etc., I was left with some little change when I arrived in London. While I was in flight on my way to London, I was thinking in my head what if I do not get a job immediately after landing to London how do I survive? Initially when I came to London for first few months, I was only eating one time in a day, could not sleep well, not just because of hunger but also hunger to achieve something big. I was doing some odd part time jobs.

Then finally, I got a proper office job in an Estate Agency. I started to gain further qualifications in real estate and got 5 certified qualifications one after other. Then this day comes around mid-2008 after the crash when employers were sacking or reducing their staffs. I faced similar threat and I was bit worried and thinking what shall I do now, stay here in London or go back home. All sorts of thoughts were going in my mind. Was my father correct? By Saying we are lower middle class people we cannot dream to become rich. The following morning I woke up with heavy heart and sat for meditation that I only used to do when I used to get upset not like regularly as I do now a days. While meditating, I am questing in my mind why did I come to UK? Shall I go back or stay here? My guru Sri Sri appears in my mind ... he said "Sumit it's not about the country. It's about you. You got to do things differently if you want different result." I decided in that moment I will do things differently now. I sat down and thought what skills do I have, Post-graduation degree in finance, Qualified Surveyor and legally sound personality who fought over 100s of cases in court, tribunal, high court etc. I decided to set up a consultancy business. With my multi-skill of finance, legal and property skills I was helping my investors clients to buy properties arranging funding for them. Slowly things started to change one by one, and I was getting good at what I was doing day by day. I was helping my investor clients to build millions of pound worth portfolio. I was nominated for best negotiator award. I was one of the surveyors who challenged and took deviation against some precedent cases like sportily V Cadagon and won. I defeated Canterbury council on a prohibition order made for 10 sq. meter studio flat which is probably the smallest self-containted unit you could have ever seen in UK, and many more record-breaking cases. One day I attended a property seminar watching the presenter explaining about few investment strategies. And while listening them, I was like oh yes on my Croydon deal I used this strategy and on that Brixton deal I used this strategy. I found that these property trainner are making lots of money teaching about property investment strategies and they do not know various strategies that I know like adding value to property without even physically touching the property, creatively buying from auctions etc. Because I can do finance and tax planning and I am legally sound, I can go extra mile comparatively. Then I become more creative, I decided not to ask some of my clients for fee whom I was getting great BMV and development potential deals but I started to ask them share in profit or equity in property. By doing so soon in less than 15 months, I found myself financial free, having a multi-million pound worth property portfolio without using any of my own money. In additional to that I helped many of my investor partners to build their multi-million pound property portfolio. I phoned my dad and said "Dad, we do not need money to fulfil our dreams, we need to be resourceful, determined and laser focused."

I started to share with my friends and clients some of my work experience and successful deals that I did. And I found they were getting impressed with performance and they asked me "can you teach us these investment strategies". I said yes sure and then I decided to educate others to do the same what I have done. With over 17 years of experience and multi-skilled I designed various training programs, books and courses to help people to achieve financial freedom and be successful. My training programs not only help my students / mentee to build their property portfolio but also teach them soft skills to empower their life. I designed some very easy steps SYSTEM, it's as easy as I make the cake in front of you and you can see me doing and then you just follow my recipe to get the same result. "SUCCESS LEAVES CLUES"

"WHY FIT IN, WHEN YOU WERE BORN TO STAND OUT"

CHAPTER 1: INTRODUCTION

"People with goals succeed because they know where they're going." — Earl Nightingale

If you are reading this book, chances are you have already started your own business or investment, or perhaps you are still gathering information in order to take that first step. But let me ask you a few questions: What do you want to get by investing into property? Do you want financial freedom? The ability to spend your time and money in the way you want rather than being tied to your regular 9 to 5 (but you always end up staying until 8) job?

Do you want to be the millionaire? I assume your answer must be yes. Why not, everyone likes to become millionaire but who actually accomplish those desires.

Why is that? The answer is simple: Most people do not apply six very common principles to their efforts when buying and selling property:

1. If you expect to have someone else do all of the work for you, do not expect that you will receive all of the rewards—**learn what to do and then get it done!**

2. Don't believe everything that you read or that you are told, unless you check it out for yourself—**you must be self-sufficient!**

3. If you don't have a map to get you where you want to go, you probably won't ever get there—**you must have a plan!**

4. If you do not ask for a better deal, you probably won't get it—**so always ask**

5. Those that snooze will lose and you cannot wait. Once you know what to do—**you must go out and make it happen!**

6. And most important—never forget! It does not take money to make money, it takes a deal to make money.

I assume you would agree with me that investment is very important to be successful, then why do people refuse to invest? Perhaps they do not have enough time, knowledge or they have fear to invest.

Probably fear is only until when you have not learned how to invest in property. Once you learn the skills, you will feel more confidents to invest in property.

Here are few Property Investment Top Tips, we will learn more about them in this book

1. Always Buy from motivated sellers at BMV (below market Value)
2. Always Buy in an area that have strong demand
3. Always Buy for good cash flow
4. Always Invest for long term
5. Always maintain enough working capital
6. Always do proper due diligence
7. Always Think creatively and Add Value
8. Always Leverage with other's money, time and experience
9. Always Make a team of professional people
10. Always keep up to date with latest legislation

Before we go further, I want you to understand few basics first. It is good to get the foundation level develop first before we look to develop anything.

✓ Clearly Identify Exactly What You Want to Achieve

Everyone has dreams. Unfortunately, most people never achieve much, if any, of what they dream. Why do you suppose that is?

As a seminar instructor, for many years I have travelled many countries around the world and had the opportunity to spend time helping many people build fortunes in real estate. In most respects, these people are just like many of you reading this book. In their lives, they had done many of the things that you do every day. They went to work, they cooked, they went to sports, they took the kids to school, they went to the health club, and they shopped for groceries.... Sound familiar, right?

However, ultimately, there is a difference between the people who become very successful and the rest of the world. Successful people are successful because they do the things they like the most. The most! Let me explain. People go to work day after day and many of them don't really care for their jobs. The job is not what they most like to do. Frankly, almost all of them would rather be doing something different, be paid more, have more time off, have better benefits, have more freedom—and the list goes on and on. So why do they stay where they are? The answer can be explained in three words: security, procrastination, and fear!

- ✓ Security because they at least have a job and don't really have to make a change.
- ✓ Procrastination because they want to change, but never quite gets around to it.
- ✓ Fear because they might be worse off if they do make a change.

Let me ask you few questions?

Are they really secure? What's the security in job? How many companies have closed their doors? How many thousands of people have lost their jobs?

Remember this: Your own personal security can only exist when you can independently generate whatever income you desire and your future is totally in your control. And what could be the biggest fear in life beyond death. We all came empty handed and we all will die without taking anything with us. Why not live the life fully, use all the resources and perform the way the world will remember us.

"Living life fully is like a roller coaster ride. There is a whirling, spinning, fast-paced perceptions, and adventure! If you are tense and holding on tight, resisting each turn, you will

feel exhausted and sick at the end. But if you can relax and have faith that the builder of the ride made it for your fun and safety, then you feel thrilled, energized, and joyful!"

GOALS — The Most Valuable Building Blocks

"Goal setting," you groan, "not that again. Every time I read a book or watch a video or go to a seminar, they talk about how important it is to set goals."

Yes, and once again, I will tell you what you have already heard 10 or 100 or 1000 times: Setting concise but flexible goals, writing them down, continually reviewing those goals, and measuring your accomplishments is critical to your own success!

- ✓ Like it or not, it is an absolute necessity. Right now is a good time to begin asking yourself: What exactly do I want to achieve out of this new real estate investment book?
- ✓ Do you want to build an on-going, income-generating business at which you can work full time?
- ✓ Do you want to keep your current job and begin buying and selling periodically for either additional income or a more fruitful retirement?

- ✓ Do you simply want to become a real estate mogul and buy and hold as many properties as possible to secure your future?
- ✓ Do you just want to buy your first house?

Identifying your goals is very important for many reasons. Most importantly, because you will learn many, many techniques from this book, it is important that you utilize the information that will best suit your needs and desires. It may take you years to utilize every method that will be shown to you. Concentrating on a specific plan and specific methods will provide the best results. As you become more and more knowledgeable and proficient with the techniques, the entire process will become less cumbersome and you will be able to branch out and use other methods.

However, remember that your goals also need to be reasonable and flexible. Reasonable, in that you must honestly evaluate the time and resources that you have to put into your own property investing venture. Flexible, because you may start out with a goal to only buy your first house and find that the process was so easy that you want to buy several more. Setting the goals, measuring your achievements, and moving the bar up to the next level is the progression of success in nearly every venture in life. The investment goal chart will help you break down each of the actions that you will need to take to accomplish your aspirations. Note that the chart requires you to state a goal, show the action that will be required, and then break down the specific actions that will be necessary.

One example might be:

Investment Goal: To purchase two properties within 90 days
Actions:

- ✓ Search the ads for properties online and offline
- ✓ Contact a Estate Agent and have her or him searched
- ✓ Search repossessed and run down properties including proeprties going in auction room
- ✓ Drive around the area and look for "For Sale by Owner" signs
- ✓ Specific Actions: Contact a minimum of 20 sellers, do follow-up letters to sellers, and view at least six properties within a set time say within a week.

Broker contact: identify 20 potential properties and view a minimum of six properties a week or more.

Driving around and

- ✓ Identify a minimum of four sellers, view a minimum of two properties,
- ✓ offers on two properties and negotiate

By breaking down your goals in this manner, you will know the exact actions that you need to take every day to accomplish your goals.

It also is very important to segregate your goals into four categories:

1. Daily action goals
2. Short-term achievement goals
3. Mid-term achievement goals
4. Long-term success goals

Daily Action Goals

These goals can best be defined as daily, weekly, and monthly activities such as personal contacts with potential sellers, viewing properties, creating and distributing flyers, and follow-ups on potential deals— everyday activities that will be necessary for you to find and close the transactions that will allow you to achieve your short-term achievement goals. Daily action goals will become almost second nature, but you must continue to track your results or you may become scattered and disorganized. Time is your most important asset and setting and prioritizing specific daily action goals will help you to utilize your time most efficiently.

Short-Term Achievement Goals

These are those goals that you want to achieve in one year or less. These include making a monthly or annual income, paying off bills, buying one or two or three properties, taking a certain vacation, buying a new car, creating more time to spend with your family, quitting your job and working full time in real estate, etc. Short-term achievement goals are the stepping stones that move you sequentially closer to achieving your long-term success goals.

Mid-Term Achievement Goals

These are those goals that you want to achieve in two years to 5 years. Some examples of five-year mid-term success goals might be net worth of £1 million, ownership of 20 properties producing a net income of £100,000 a year etc.

Long-Term Success Goals

These are those goals that you want to achieve in 5 to 10 years. Ten-year goals can be moved up substantially, but keep in mind, things change. Your 5 to and 10 year long-term success goals need to be the most flexible.

As you gain more knowledge, experience, and confidence, you also will become smarter at setting goals and you'll find that you have a tendency to push yourself a little more than you did when you were first beginning your new venture. As I said before, as you work with the process, the easier it will become and the less complicated it will seem to you. It will be the same with your goal setting. It will become habitual and second nature. Our minds need to have clear WHY to function and achieve the goal.

We should have our clear written down goals, that you read every day before you start your day and plan what action will you take today to achieve that goal.

Once Harvard's graduate students were asked if they had set themselves any goals and if so, if they had made any plans to accomplish them

Group A: 3% had written down goals with plans to accomplish them

Group B: 13% had goals and plans in mind but with nothing written down

Group C: 84% had no goals at all

After 10 years they revisited the same group of students and the results were very clear...

Group B: Earned on average twice as much as Group C

Group A: Earned on average 10 times as much as all of Group B and Group C combined!

See the power of having a written goal.

Time—Your Most Valuable Asset

How many times have you heard someone say, "I would love to be able to have the time to do this or that or be able to go here or there, but I am so busy and have so little time that I just can't do it." Many of you have probably said or thought those same things at one time or another. But, the real truth is that there are only 24 hours in a day and we all make the time that we need or want to for the things that are the real priorities in our lives. If you want something different than what you have, you must first, and honestly, change your priorities. We all have the same amount of time each and every single day. We spend the time, we waste the time or invest the time creatively. What we do with our time is entirely up to us.

Many people enjoy looking and acting and being busy. The problem is that most people are highly unproductive, whether they are busy or not. Like any other venture, if you are to be successful in the property investment business, you must prioritize and manage your time to allow you to complete the actions that will be necessary for you to achieve your goals. Remember, a commitment of four or five hours a week might be all that is necessary for you to become a successful property investor.

Work smartly and see how you spend your time every day, record in a diary and see what are the task you can outsource to others at a cheaper rate than what you are worth. These days you can get almost anything done through others using fiverr, upwork, peopleperhour type platform. You spend your time in what is really necessary and invest your time in your personal development as much as possible.

Managing Your Time

There have been many books written on time management. Here is my simple, two-part formula for successful time management, broken into preparation and actions.

Preparation

Simplify your life. Stop doing the things that are not essential or that you really don't want or have to do the things that are getting in the way of the success that you want to achieve.

Control what people and actions get your time. Do not let other people's priorities take control of your life.

Balance your actions, and balance your life. Figure 1.2 shows a pie chart representing a sample allocation of the 24 hours in your day. This shows that you should designate allotted time for the essential activities in your life and strive to maintain that balance.

Identify and control procrastination. Learn to prioritize and focus. There is a good book called "Eat that frog" by Brian Tracy. Do not allow yourself to waste valuable time.

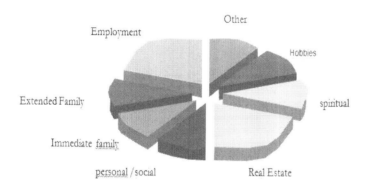

FIGURE 1.2 The pie chart shows that you must allow time for the essential activities of your life. You make your chart like this.

Before we continue

I would like to congratulate you for buying this book and more importantly for starting to read it. Would you believe that 40% of the books that are purchased are never even opened. I often meet people who say they purchased my book a year or so ago but never got round to reading it and then when they did finally read it, they wished that they had done it years ago. So my recommendation here is very simple. Read the book in full and then read it again.

I can't teach you everything and my 17 years' experience in a book in few hours, but I will expand your thinking and help you to recognise how property investing could change your life, which will in turn hopefully inspire you to take action. At the end of the day, it's down to you to take action to achieve the results you desire, but the good news is you don't have to do it on your own because that really can be hard work.

The information that I share in this book is not just theoretical. Although the content is mainly about strategies that work here in the UK, the general principle of finding and helping motivated sellers is a concept that works anywhere in the world, although factors such as financing, taxation and regulations may

of course be different in other countries.

CHAPTER 2: WHY TO INVEST IN PROPERTY

"Compounding Result is the 8th wonder of the world" – Sumit Gupta

Traditionally, a pension is simply a form of saving for retirement that has tax benefits. The income paid out to today's pensioners by the state, is funded by those who are working now. As the proportion of people over state pension age grows, the more expensive it gets.

In my opinion, it is unlikely that the state will be able to afford to support us. Probably you would be aware that relying on pension is not going to work. Unless, you do something about it now, which is why I assume you are reading this book.

You have several options for investment, few main ones are:

- ✓ You could invest in shares.
- ✓ You could invest in property.
- ✓ You could start business or similar activities to generate some extra income.

Personally I have done all the above three and I can say this with confidence that investing in property is by far better, simplest and safer.

In case, if you have not started investing until now and feel you will do in near future and this is in your "TO DO" list. Then think twice and read further the benefit of investing earlier than late. Let's first go through more in detail why we should invest and the impact of regular investment or compound. See the table below:

Let's illustrate the tremendous impact of compounding with just one simple but mind-blowing example. Two friends, Yash and John, decide to invest £250 a month. Yash gets started at age 19, keeps going for 10 years and then stops adding to this pot at age 28. In all, he's saved a total of £30,000.

Yash's money then compounds at a rate of 10% a year (10% assumed rate of growth p.a.). By the time he retires at 65, how much does he have? The answer is £1.788 million approx. (see the example spread sheet below). In other words, that modest investment of £30,000 has grown to nearly two million! Pretty stunning, huh?

His friend John gets off to a slower start. He begins investing exactly the same amount £250 a month but doesn't get started until age 27. Still, he's a disciplined guy, and he keeps investing £250 every month until he's 65 – a period of 39 years. His money also compounds at 10% a year. And the result is? When he retires at 65, he's sitting on a pot of £1.3 million approx.

Let's think about this for a moment. John invested a total of £117,000 almost four times more than the £30,000 that Yash invested. Yet Yash has ended up with an extra £463k. That's right: Yash ends up richer than John, despite the fact that he never invested a penny after the age of 28!

What explains Yash's incredible success? Simple. By starting earlier, the compound interest to be earned on his investment adds more value to his account than he could ever add on his own. By the time he reaches age 52, the compound interest on his account adds over £50,000 per year to his balance. By the time he's 59, his account is growing by more than £100,000 per year! All without adding another penny. John's total return on the money he invested is around 1,000%, whereas Yash's return is a spectacular around 6,000%. This is simply Yash started investing 8 years earlier than John.

That's the awesome power of compounding. Over time this force can turn a modest sum of money into a massive fortune. See full working below:

£250 monthly (£3000 annually) growing at 10% p.a.

Age	Yash	Amount	John	amount
Age 19	£3,000	£3,300		
Age 20	£3,000	£6,930		
Age 21	£3,000	£10,923		
Age 22	£3,000	£15,315		
Age 23	£3,000	£20,147		
Age 24	£3,000	£25,462		
Age 25	£3,000	£31,308		
Age 26	£3,000	£37,738		

Age 27	£3,000	£ 44,812	£3,000	£3,300
Age 28	£3,000	£52,594	£3,000	£6,930
Age 29		£57,853	£3,000	£10,923
Age 30		£63,638	£3,000	£15,315
Age 31		£70,002	£3,000	£20,147
Age 32		£77,002	£3,000	£25,462
Age 33		£84,702	£3,000	£31,308
Age 34		£93,173	£3,000	£37,738
Age 35		£102,490	£3,000	£ 44,812
Age 36		£112,739	£3,000	£52,594
Age 37		£124,013	£3,000	£61,153
Age 38		£136,414	£3,000	£70,568
Age 39		£150,055	£3,000	£80,925
Age 40		£165,061	£3,000	£92,317
Age 41		£181,567	£3,000	£104,849
Age 42		£199,724	£3,000	£118,634
Age 43		£219,696	£3,000	£133,798

Age 44	£241,666	£3,000	£150,477
Age 45	£265,832	£3,000	£168,825
Age 46	£292,416	£3,000	£189,007
Age 47	£321,657	£3,000	£211.208
Age 48	£353,823	£3,000	£235,629
Age 49	£389,205	£3,000	£262,492
Age 50	£428,126	£3,000	£292,412
Age 51	£470,938	£3,000	£324,545
Age 52	£518,032	£3,000	£360,300
Age 53	£569,835	£3,000	£399,630
Age 54	£626,819	£3,000	£442,893
Age 55	£689,500	£3,000	£490,482
Age 56	£758,451	£3,000	£542,830
Age 57	£834,296	£3,000	£600,413
Age 58	£917,725	£3,000	£663,755
Age 59	£1,009,498	£3,000	£733,430
Age 60	£1,110,447	£3,000	£810,073

Age 61	£1,221,492	£3,000	£894,380
Age 62	£1,343,641	£3,000	£987,118
Age 63	£1,478,00647	£3,000	£1.089,130
Age 64	£1,625,806	£3,000	£1,202,343

Age 65	**£1,788,387**	**£3,000**	**£1,324,778**

Advantage of investing early:	**£463,609**

But you know what's amazing? Most people never take full advantage of this secret that's lying in full view, this wealth-building miracle that's sitting there right in front of their eyes. Instead, they continue to believe that they can earn their way to become rich. It's a common misperception this belief that, if you earned income is big enough, you'll become financially free.

The truth is, it's not that simple. We've all read stories about movie stars, musicians and athletes who earned more money yet ended up broke because they didn't know how to invest and manage wealth. You may have heard many examples of such people. Even the King of Pop, Michel Jackson, who reportedly signed a recording contract worth almost $1 billion and sold more than 750 million records, supposedly owed more than $300 million upon his death in 2009.

The lesson? You're never going to earn your way to financial freedom. The real route to riches is to set aside a portion of your money and invest it, so that is compounded over many years. That's how you become wealthy while you sleep. That's how you make money work for you instead of you working for money. That's how you achieve true financial freedom. Depending where you invest, your investment can grow even faster than 10% p.a. And good thing is if you invest in property by leveraging well using banks loan and other people money the growths are even faster.

I have been asked many times by people why should we invest in property. And I had explained this why property was such a compelling investment strategy over other asset classes.

So what are some of the reasons why you should invest in property?

Leverage

Leverage is simply utilising debt to finance the acquisition of an asset. In property, one can use leverage not only as a means of increasing the return on equity invested through obtaining a mortgage. This is something that cannot be done with investing in other asset classes e.g. trading stocks and shares or investing money in savings accounts and relying on bank interest. Leverage enables investors invest less money to generate a greater return on investment (ROI). If you go to a bank and ask for £200,000 loan to buy the property more likely, you will get the money funded by the bank as long as everything else is in order such as you have some deposit and good credit etc. Even good thing is if you have not got deposit or good credit you can take this from someone else. And leverage with their money and their credit. However, if you go to a bank and ask for £200,000 loan to invest in stock market, you know the answer, right?

Capital growth

They say property doubles in value every seven to ten years. This isn't necessarily true in all circumstances but property has certainly seen a rise for the last 5-10 years. And if you see the UK house price index or any other countries real estate graphs, you will find the growth is significant. Therefore, a investor's property which initially cost £200,000 in 2012 would now be worth circa £350,000. With a monthly rental income on top of this, it certainly acts as a perpetual advantage to investing in property.

Gearing

Following on from leverage, one facility available to property investors is the ability to 'gear' your portfolio. To explain, this is where one may have £100,000 available and one option is to invest all this money in one property worth £100,000. Alternatively, through gearing, the same £100,000 could be utilized to buy 4 properties at down payment of £25,000 each with 4 buy to let mortgages. This figures I am using for example purpose only, obviously there will be some cost on top and stamp duty etc. but understand this as concept. With the above example in mind, if property prices increase in that area in a year by 25%, should the investor had bought one property for £100,000, his/her property portfolio would now be worth £125,000. However had the investor used the same equity and invested in four properties their portfolio would now be worth £500,000 (4 x £125,000). Therefore there are great returns to be had in multiple property investment.

Interest rates at an all-time low to date, interest rates are incredibly low and the Bank of England base rate currently sits at 0.25% with more competition in the buy-to-let lenders market than ever, as people buy for a piece of the pie. With servicing mortgage debt being so low, this act as a great opportunity for landlords to re-finance their portfolio, release more equity, purchase additional properties and obtain a greater return.

Tangible/physical asset

Over stocks and shares and other forms of investment, from experience, there is something quite comforting about having an asset that you can touch and feel over something electronic. You know where your property is and know it won't go anywhere! And you can add value to it and control it to a large extend.

Opportunity to add value

There are plenty of opportunities to add value whether it is a refurb project or a lease extension, which are not available in other asset classes. Again using a rough example, you may be able to buy a property which requires some work doing, and increase its value once the works is done. You may struggle to purchase other investments at a reduced price, make them better and resell them for a higher price.

Take away

Impact of compound is like the 8th wonder of the world.

Investment is the only route to make money work for you rather than you work of money.

CHAPTER 3: MAKE YOUR POWER TEAM AND GATHER YOUR PERSONAL RESOURCES

"Do not wait; the time will never be 'just right.' Start where you stand, and work with whatever tools you may have at your command, and better tools will be found as you go along." —

Napoleon Hill

Where Is Your Starting Line?

In my seminars, I reach a point where I say to everyone, "Okay, now we're going to take inventory of each of your personal resources." Without fail, someone will utter, "What resources?" or "This won't take long," or the best one, "I have no resources, I spent my last £100 to come to the seminar!"

Everyone always laughs, but often the people who made the remarks stated exactly what they believed to be the truth—they believed that they had no resources. However, if you look around, you'll see that we live in a world abundant with resources for success:

- ✓ Do you have access to a computer or the Internet?
- ✓ Do you have access to a telephone and mobile?
- ✓ Do you have any estate agents offices in your city?
- ✓ Do you have a local newspaper, property magazine?

There may be many other things that you would have access to.

If you answered yes to any one of these questions, and you have this book to guide you, you have all the resources necessary to make you as rich as you wish to be. Most of you answered yes to all of the questions and if you are thinking, that increases your chances for even greater success, you are right. The question becomes: How do you use those resources that are available to you? The answer is very simple: You must take the right actions, in the right order, at the right time. So, what are the right actions, what is the right order, and when is the right time?

The Basic Action Plan

The order of action that you must adhere to is actually very straight- forward. Everything that you will learn in this book is based on the following basic action plan. You must:

- ✓ Identify potential properties and sellers
- ✓ Choose the best prospects from your list of potentials
- ✓ Always be making contacts with potential sellers
- ✓ Negotiate a win-win transaction for you and the seller
- ✓ Find the money to fund the deal
- ✓ Use all resources to close the transaction

✓ Never forget to follow up on all commitments and promises

✓ Don't stop use, exchange, or lose the cash

It is imperative that you follow each and every one of these actions. If you try to skip steps, attempting to move ahead or make things happen more quickly, you may find yourself wasting a lot of time, not closing any transactions, and never making any money. Remember there is no shortcut to make money.

How do you remember every step? Very simple. You memorize them and you use them every day. If you look at the first letter of each action step mentioned above, you will find that it spells out "I CAN FUND," which is exactly what you will do.

You Can Make Deals with What You Have or Don't Have

If I offered to sell you a diamond that was perfect in colour and clarity and was just over three carats for, let's say, £2,000? Most of you are not diamond experts or have many contacts in the field of fine gems, but you would probably recognize that this is a deal you might not want to pass up. If you did your homework, determined that the diamond was real and that it had a wholesale market value of over £40,000, and identified that there were buyers who would purchase the stone for at least half of the value, my guess is that you would probably make a concerted effort to come up with the £2,000 and put the deal together. Am I right?

Even though you don't have a great deal of money or knowledge, you know that this is a deal that you just can't pass up. Now, let me ask you another question. If you went to your best friend, mother, father, sister, brother, neighbour, co-worker, or anyone else and said, "I want to borrow £2,000 and I'll pay you back as soon as I can," do you believe that you might have some difficulty getting the money?

However, if you went to those same people with all of the information about the diamond transaction, put together in a concise and understandable form, including offers to purchase from gem buyers, and you offered to pay back £3,000 in 60 days or less, for the £2,000 loan, would you have more interest from the potential lenders? Of course you would!

Visit my website www.propertyexpertsacademy.com

and download free property deal analyser. Everything is done for you and you can adjust it according to the deal & +situation.

It Does Not Take Your Money to Make Money

There Are Professionals Available to Help You—Use Them!

Let's face it. You can't be an expert in every area relating to real estate or any other investment field. I have been involved in the business from just about every aspect imaginable for over 17 years and I still learn something nearly every day. As much as I try to be self-reliant and independent, I have learned that becoming successful in the real estate investment business must be a team effort. Fortunately, there are a lot of experts out there that will want to be part of your team.

Why is that, you ask? Because, while they are helping you to make a lot of money, you are going to be helping them to make a lot of money too.

"I discovered a long time ago that if I helped enough people get what they wanted, I would always get what I wanted and I would never have to worry." - Tony Robins

Putting Your Investment Team Together

While preparing for one of my seminar, I had the opportunity to interview dozens of agents, brokers, investors, and entrepreneurs who had started with virtually nothing and were all self-made multimillionaires. These success superstars all had many things in common, but the aspect that stood out more than any other was the fact that every one of them recognized that if you want to achieve greatness, happiness, and success, you must have a superstar team surrounding you every day of your life.

You cannot do it alone. And frankly, why would you want to? There are only so many hours in a day, there is only so much liability that you can carry on your own, there is only so much that you can know, there are only so many places that you can be in one day, and there are only so many phone calls that you personally can make. Let's face it. You need help! So, where do you get the help that you need? Like everything else in life, you ask for it!

Here is the process you need to follow to build your own investment team.

1.Start with the people who will help you to get the deals. The real estate brokers and agents, architects, and anyone else who can help you find a good property to purchase.

2.Create a good banking relationship. Even if you have bad credit and you are very short of funds, find a banker who will believe in you and help you to start, or restart, a joint venture partner to fill this gap. Make them believe in you.

3.Develop a relationship with professionals who can guide you when you need assistance: a solicitor, an accountant, a tax expert, a surveyor, an appraiser, a property manager, an insurance

CHAPTER 4: ANALYSING THE MARKET AND HOW TO FIND THE DEALS

This is very important part as it is with nearly any business, it is critical that you have a good understanding of the marketplace in which you have decided to work. As you begin to search for properties, your time will become more and more valuable and it will be critical that you spend your hours prudently. Your decisions about properties and your actions to make offers must be done quickly and efficiently for you to become successful and reach your goals.

What Is the Process?

As I have discussed previously in several sections of this book, it is important to have a detailed and specific plan when it comes time to begin searching for the areas in neighbourhoods in which you are interested, as well as the properties that you'll ultimately purchase. The process of finding the right properties at the right price involves a simple five-step method that if followed exactly will produce outstanding results:

✓ Find the area
✓ Find the properties that might be for sale

- ✓ Identify and go after the sellers who have the properties you want
- ✓ Make an offer, work through negotiations, and get an accepted offer
- ✓ Close the transaction and make the move
- ✓ Finding the Best Areas, Neighbourhoods, and Properties

Most new investors start off looking for cheap of low-end properties. There are several reasons that most of these investors choose this route. New investors, for the most part, are afraid that if they make a mistake on a more expensive investment, they may not be able to recover as quickly as they might with a less expensive property.

As you begin to look at properties as potential investments, I suggest that you divide the potential investments into five categories:

Level 1: Low-end, cheap, and maybe needing a lot of work

Level 2: Moderately inexpensive

Level 3: Mid-level

Level 4: Expensive

Level 5: Very expensive

Figure 1.3 will help you to remember the levels.

there will be many transactions where your success depends not on the size or price of the property, but on the type of transaction that you can structure. However, for the most part, I have found that beginning investors seem to be better served starting their investment careers with Level 2, moderately inexpensive properties.

Level 5 Very Expensive— limited availability

Level 4 Expensive— more readily available than Level 5

Level 3 Mid-Level—average availability

Level 2 Moderately inexpensive readily available

Level 1 Low-end, least expensive— most readily available

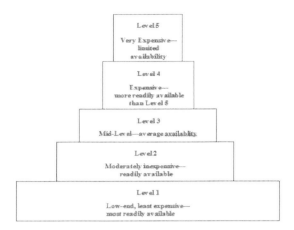

FIGURE 1.3 Levels of price and property availability.

There are a number of reasons why Level 2 properties seem to work out best for new investors:

- ✓ Level 2 properties are easy to find.

- ✓ Level 2 properties tend to have the most comparables.

- ✓ Level 2 properties are usually owned by sellers who must deal with common personal and economic problems such as job loss, bankruptcy, and divorce.

- ✓ Level 2 properties in need of basic, cosmetic repairs are usually easy to locate.

- ✓ Level 2 properties often have sellers who can be flexible and accommodating for a buyer.

- ✓ Level 2 properties have a higher turnover rate than most other levels.

- ✓ Level 2 properties provide opportunities ranging from one- to four-family occupancy, often decreasing the cost per unit and thereby increasing the income and sale potential for the investor.

- ✓ Level 2 properties have very good long-term wealth-building potential, as well as short-term income possibilities.

What Are the Most Common Mistakes?

One of the most common mistakes made by new investors is to buy a dilapidated, Level 1 property that requires an enormous amount of work to bring it to a state where it can be rented or sold.

If an investor in a Level 1 property has the experience, ability, and time to do the repairs, this type of property can generate enormous profits. However, if the investor does not have those specific abilities, the profits can be greatly depleted and the value of the investment can drop dramatically.

If your goal is to generate a monthly income and you are going to work full-time in the real estate business and you have the abilities to do major repairs, Level 1 properties may work for you. However, if you are looking for long-term wealth or a better retirement from your part time property investment, my suggestion is that you work more with Level 2 and Level 3 properties.

Another common mistake of new investors is to try to make a large profit on every property they buy. Many of these investors are out to make their whole fortune or retirement on one deal and they try to buy the biggest, highest-priced property that they can get their hands on. Many times that approach ends up in disaster because the investor doesn't't have the ability and experience to ultimately make the deal work. However once you have got great experience you may want to do bigger deals.

Making the Right Choices

You may have heard in my seminar or my blog post, I discussed the importance of investors having a solid knowledge of an entire area before they start making the decisions about which neighbourhoods they were going to invest in. It should go without saying that if in an overall area, unemployment is increasing, employers are laying off workers and closing their businesses, and the general economy in an area is declining, that might not be the best marketplace for an investor to be working.

Tracking Your Research—Developing and Using a Property Search Log

Developing and using a property search log is the most important step in beginning your area and property searches. After you have chosen the area(s) in which you are interested in investing, you will begin looking at specific properties, probably first on the Internet and then in person. What you must remember is that your search for the right properties will be ongoing. You must not forget that you may view 40 or 50 or even 100 properties before you make offers. For all of the properties that you view that are potentials, it will be critical for you to have detailed information pages and photographs so you will be able to remember all of the aspects of those individual properties. The fact is, after you have seen only about 10 properties, they will all begin to blend together in your mind.

Each time that you buy a property, you must do so with selling in mind. Although, you may buy 20, 30 or 100 properties before you ever sell one, you want to always be sure that you are as property liquid as is possible. By property liquid I mean that every property you own could be easily liquidated or sold in nearly any market and in a short period of time.

Twenty great ways to find the property deals

1. London Gazette
2. Estate agents
3. Auctioneers
4. Newspapers
5. Leaflets
6. Postcards
7. Lead websites
8. Your own websites
9. Social media
10. References or Word of mouth
11. Driving or Walking on the streets
12. Networking meetings
13. Professional advisors like surveyors, Architect etc
14. Redundancy advisors
15. Bank or other lenders
16. Private Landlords
17. Other investors unwanted deals
18. Derelict properties
19. Property forums
20. Debt forums

CHAPTER 5: NEGOTIATION TECHNIQUES THAT CREATE WIN-WIN SITUATION

"The most important trip you may take in life is meeting people half way." – Henry Boyle

B eing a good negotiator can be the difference between being able to structure a fair deal or a terrific deal. Your own personal negotiation skills will be extremely important to your financial success in real estate investment.

Important Factors to Remember When Negotiating

Negotiating must become second nature. You must be able to move into a negotiation mode immediately when you come in contact with someone with whom you might eventually do business, whether you have prepared specifically for that negotiation or not. You must be knowledgeable and ready to do business at all times. In all negotiations, there are a few factors that you should understand:

✓ You must establish trust and credibility with every person with whom you are negotiating. You must learn to establish that trust in a very short period of time.

✓ As much as possible, you must quickly develop a rapport with every person with whom you are negotiating. You must seek to find a common ground whereby you and every other person with whom you're dealing is comfortable. That common ground may or may not be the real estate on which you are negotiating. Remember, musician like to talk about music, fishermen like to talk about fishing, car lover like to talk about cars, etc. Many times, what you say is not as important as how you say it.

✓ You must take the time to discover the needs and the desires of the people with whom you're negotiating and then move to satisfy those needs and desires. Patience and thoroughness are key aspects of that process.

✓ You must be careful not to display a great deal of self-interest. It is important in a win-win situation that all parties are willing to work to meet the needs of everyone involved in the transaction, and your demeanour, attitude and actions should lend themselves to that end.

✓ You must keep in mind that the party with whom you are negotiating must have at least as much desire to complete the transaction as you have or you are probably wasting your time.

✓ You must keep emotion out of your negotiations as much as possible. If you feel pressure or uneasiness starting to develop, it is better to back off and continue the negotiations at a later time.

✓ Never make assumptions for which you have no basis in fact. Assuming that a seller will not be interested in assisting in the financing, accepting a low down payment, taking a lesser price for their property, etc., are common assumptions made by new investors. Those assumptions can kill a transaction that otherwise might have gone together with a little positive effort.

✓ Be extremely careful saying things that are critical or negative about the property on which you are negotiating. The thinking by some investors that a great deal of criticism of a particular property, when dealing with a seller, will result in a better deal on the property is definitely flawed thinking.

✓ Keep your negotiations focused on the terms that matter most. Do not get side tracked by superfluous items that may cloud the important issues. That said, there are times when you will use nonessential items to offset the more important terms and issues in a transaction.

✓ Concentrate your efforts on identifying and solving the problems of the other parties to the transaction, while at the same time meeting your own needs and desires.

✓ Most important of all—you must be persistent. Through all levels of your negotiations, make sure that you are unrelenting in your effort to get the deal you want.

The First Impression Is the Most Important

It is extremely important that your first meeting with a seller goes well if there are to be any potential future negotiations. It is always best if the first contact be very low-key and not necessarily gets into the specifics of the transaction. Your goal in the first meeting will be to accomplish five things:

1. Collect as much information as possible about the property and the seller and identify any needs and problems that may exist with either the property or the

seller. These needs and problem areas will help you to prepare an offer that will be suitable to you and the seller.

2. Establish a rapport and working relationship with the seller.

3. Set the stage for the next meeting when you will begin to discuss terms for the purchase of the property.

4. Establish a trust with the seller and tell him or her exactly how and when your next contact will occur.

5. Show special attention to the seller's needs, interests, and desires.

Usually, after the first meeting with a seller, you will know if there is a possibility that you may be able to put the transaction together. However, sometimes the first meeting will not provide you with enough information to allow you to make a decision as to how you want to structure an offer. If you feel that you will require more information, make sure that you leave the seller with the understanding that you will be contacting him or her for whatever information you require before you make your buying decision.

The most important aspect of the first contact, from your point of view as an investor, is to measure the seller's need and desire to liquidate the property. This aspect is most important for two reasons. You will base the terms of your offer partially on that need and desire, and you can measure the urgency with which you need to develop your offer. Obviously, if a seller is in foreclosure and there are only three days left in the redemption period, the seller is going to be highly motivated and want to see some resolution for the problem in a very short period of time.

Identifying the Most Important Topics of Negotiation

The most important topics of negotiation are fairly easy for you to identify as an investor:

Price for property

Terms of sale: Who gets what, for what, and within what time frame; include all conditions, contingencies, and exceptions

The what ifs: Everything that can, might, or will occur during the term of the transaction; cover all the bases

As easy as it is to identify the most important topics of negotiation for the investor, it may be equally as difficult to identify those important topics for a seller. That is why it is critically important to identify the problems, needs, and desires of the seller as early as possible in the negotiations.

The 10 Rules for Proper Negotiation—Memorize Them

1. Listen first—then talk.

Being a good listener is the only way you will ever become a good negotiator. You must learn to collect the pertinent data and information from the person with whom you are negotiating, analyses that data and information, and then provides a response. The first dictum of negotiating:

2. He who offers first, loses

We have had hundreds of thousands of investors, brokers, agents, mortgage lenders, and other people attend our programs. It never ceases to amaze me that, as often as I have said it, written it, and proclaimed it, "Listen first—then talk," this is still the hardest rule for everyone to remember and follow. Therefore, I will share with you a short story that came from one of our long-time students that will help you to remember the importance of this rule. He offered for a property to a direct vendor £200,000 without asking what vendor wants, later on he realized that property was in market for £190,000 only.

3. Always negotiate in person

Eye to eye is the only way you will ever be able to get the feel for the seller's true desires, and it is the best way for you to build a rapport with that seller. Also, avoid written negotiations except in counteroffer situations, and never negotiate terms and intricate details over the telephone.

4. Use all of the terms of the offer to achieve what is most important to you

You must remember that there are six areas of negotiation that will be most important in almost every transaction. They are: **price, down payment, interest rate, payments, dates, and terms.** If keeping the payment low so you can have a cash flow from the property is most important, you can use a combination of price, down payment, interest rate, dates, and terms to facilitate your receiving the payments you are seeking. If you are looking for the best price possible, you could use down payment, interest rate, payments, dates, and terms to achieve that.

5. Use nonrequisite terms during negotiations whenever possible

As an example, if you are negotiating on a 3 bedroom typical Victorian house, you might ask the seller to resurface the entire parking area, knowing fully well that some minor repairs to the surface would be adequate. If the seller knows that the complete resurfacing would be £8,000 to £10,000 and you are willing to compromise and save the seller a portion of that cost, in the mind of that seller you have made a concession and he or she may feel obligated to compromise on terms that are truly more important to you, such as price or down payment.

If you give up five or six non-requisite items during a negotiation, the seller will have less problem conforming to your wishes with regard to one or more terms that truly have more importance to you.

6. Be patient

In any negotiations, it will usually take time for the other parties to understand and accept your point of view. Do not try to hurry, but instead allow the seller to express his or her needs, desires, and point of view and adapt your presentation to the things that are most important to the seller. You may need to explain certain benefits of the transaction, again and again, before the seller will understand.

7. Ask questions and paraphrase the answers back to the seller if you do not understand the seller's motivation.

The best way to build a seller's trust is to identify exactly what makes that seller click, what he or she is truly trying to achieve out of the sale. As you would note, by asking the right questions in the proper manner, you can easily clarify the seller's concerns and needs and better under- stand how you need to structure an offer that will satisfy that seller's needs.

8. Continually identify the value of the terms your offer.

Throughout all of your negotiations you must continually identify for the parties with whom you are negotiating all of the benefits they will be receiving by accepting your offer. In other words, if sellers are receiving the cash they need to handle any current financial issues they may have, monthly payments that will help with their ongoing economic dilemma, the relief of the pressure of owning a property, removing the obligation of the sellers to make repairs on the property, etc., the value of these items is their motivation. You need to mention those things at every opportunity during the negotiation.

9. KISS

As you may have heard keep it simple stupid (KISS), is very appropriate when it comes to all levels of negotiation, especially with non-professional property owners. The more simply that your offers can be prepared, the easier the negotiations will be. That is not to say that you needn't be thorough with your paperwork and all other aspects of the transaction.

10. Have alternatives in mind at all times

Just as you will have baselines pre-established before you meet with a potential seller, you also should have in mind several alternative ways that you might be able to structure a transaction if you find the seller to be flexible and accommodating.

Nearly all of the most effective negotiators that I have worked with over the past 17 years have used somewhat the same technique or formula that I use when it comes to reaching agreement on the terms and stipulations of a property transaction. Here is the most comfortable and effective scenario that I have found when it comes to negotiating:

1. I prepare a list of absolutes that I feel are absolutely necessary for me to be able to put the deal together.

Those absolutes usually include price, down payment, and monthly payments in case of lease option strategies, and may also include other stipulations with regard to the terms or the property itself.

2. I prepare a second list of preferred items that I would really prefer to have included in the transaction, but that are not as essential as the absolutes and can be used as needed during the negotiation process.

3. I prepare a list of non-requisite items that are not essential and do not have much bearing on whether or not I will be able to structure a transaction with the seller or person with whom I am negotiating. As mentioned earlier, these non-requisite items can become very important when it comes down to who gets what and who gives up what.

Give it a shot: what do you have to lose? When you have analysed a seller's needs and desires and you feel you are in tune with what the seller is trying to achieve, don't be afraid to make an offer that only comes close to giving the seller what he or she wants. You may be very surprised at how many times you will get a positive response. If nothing else, the shot-in-the-dark offer will at least give you an idea of how stringent the seller is going to be on his or her requirements.

Other Important Factors Pertaining to Negotiation

1. Be sure that all owners or parties to the negotiation are present at the time of negotiation.

2. Do not ask for too much at any one time. Get approval on each term or requirement as you move through the negotiation. Do not hit them with everything at once.

3. Do not try to use scare tactics. There is no need to use unethical methods to achieve what can be done legally and honestly.

4. Always present your offers back to front. Start with the many items that you are giving away and that benefit the seller and work up to the most important terms, which are usually price and down payment.

5. Always make your offer prices uneven numbers, such as £139,330, instead of £140,000. The seller will believe that you have structured the offer more exactly to meet his or her needs.

6. If you run into a problem in the negotiations that could be a deal breaker, ask for time to consult with a third party such as a solicitor or an accountant. Make the bad guy someone other than yourself.

7. Make sure that there is symmetry between your words and your actions. Body language can be a dead giveaway if you are feeling uncomfortable.

8. Never allow a seller more than few days to accept your offer. So set a deadline showing some reason for your offer.

9. Always be cool. Never let your emotions show if you begin to feel uncomfortable. Keep your poker face on and maintain the approach that you will get a win-win deal for everyone or it does not bother you in the least to walk away.

10. Make your signature pitch and practice, you may be 70 to 80% good in it initially but as you implement few times you would keep getting better.

CHAPTER 6: YOU DO NOT HAVE TO DO EVERYTHING YOURSELF (LEARN LEVERAGE)

"Your workforce is your most valuable asset. The knowledge and skills they have represent the fuel that drives the engine of business, and you can leverage that knowledge". Harvey

Mackay

Building Property portfolio is a team work, you cannot do everything yourself, neither you should try to do it all. You should do what you are good at and get the rest of the job done through others.

Successful business people know that they cannot do everything on their own and they hire people who are great at the things that they are not so good at.

Your power team is made up of the professionals around you that you use in the day to day running of your business.

Letting agent- your letting agent will be invaluable for helping you evaluate the lettability of properties you are looking at and then to let and manage those properties that you decide to add to your portfolio.

THE ULTIMATE GUIDE TO PROPERTY INVESTMENT
HOW TO MAKE BIG MONEY

Property solicitor / conveyancer - A capable property solicitor will ensure the smooth handling of your property transactions, if they are experienced in creative property strategies.

Property valuer / surveyor - A flexible property valuer will be an important member of your team if you are buying and selling or sourcing property for other investors as you'll need to get mortgage valuations, or Homebuyers Reports. visit surveyors at our partner site at www.global-property-consulting.com

Property investment coach - Many successful investors are now deciding to add a property mentor to their team to multiply their results and keep their property business on the right track. Visit our website www.propertyexpertsacademy.com if you like to enrol for mentorship.

Property accountant - An accountant experienced in the field of property will see that as much of your hard earned profits as possible are not swiped by the tax man at the end of the year! Don't forget that many questions about property tax can be answered by HMRC, without having to pay a professional!

Investment mortgage broker - A specialist investment mortgage broker will search the ever changing finance market for the best products to fund your deals and fight your corner when things go wrong.

Bridging finance company - If you are looking for short term finance then a good bridger will be very useful

Investment property insurance broker - Whether you're insuring a rental property or a house, a good broker will be able to source the best product for the purpose

Tradesmen - Efficient and reliable tradesmen will be essential to see to refurbishment works, routine maintenance, gas safety checks, electrical safety checks etc.

Outsource some of your work!

Almost any type of work can be outsourced to someone at much cheaper price. While these are going to be the main members of a property team, when your property business grows to a certain size, you will want to concentrate on the bits of it that you are good at and get someone else to do the stuff you're not so good at or do not enjoy doing.

CHAPTER 7: ELEVEN SUCCESSFUL PROPERTY INVESTMENT STRATEGIES

There are various property investments strategies. Here I am going to explain you about few main successful S.T.R.A.T.E.G.I.E.S ™ that I teach my student and mentees.

- ✓ S – Sell leads (deal packaging)
- ✓ T- Title splitting
- ✓ R- Rent to Rent
- ✓ A- Auction purchase using special techniques
- ✓ T- To Let (buy to Let)
- ✓ E- Exchange with delay completion
- ✓ G- Get control by taking option or lease option
- ✓ Internal Conversion including commercial conversion
- ✓ E- Extra accommodation for multiple tenants (HMO)
- ✓ S- Service Accommodation and Holiday let

Let's explore little more about each of the above S.T.R.A.T.E.G.I.E.S ™. However each of the above strategies are so important and need detail understanding that's why I have designed workshop for each of the above strategies from 1 day to 3 days workshop. Where one can learn all of these strategies more in details with practical approach.

S – Sell leads or deal packaging

This is a powerful strategy to build an income from property by sourcing property deals and then selling them to investors for a lump sum finder's fee. You can earn an average of anywhere between £2,000 – £10,000 in fees per property deal so it doesn't't take many to replace a full time income.

The kind of deals that are sourced by deal packagers are Rent to Rent, Below Market Value and Lease Option properties and the fee commanded usually varies according to the length of the term. The longer the lease option you have you can get demand more fee.

The great thing about deal packaging is you don't need a fortune to get started, just great training, determination and consistent action is certain to bring you financial rewards

T- Title splitting

A creative investment strategy becoming more and more popular these days is Title Splitting, where you purchase a property and literally split it into two, three or more properties to rent out or re-sell. This can be a complicated process and you must first do extensive due diligence and research, speak to the local council, planning officer, prepare a pre app and make sure your numbers are always right.

Top tips for Title Splits:

- ✓ Speak to the local councils
- ✓ Speak to a surveyor
- ✓ Speak to a Planning officer
- ✓ Speak to at least 3 or 4 estate agents
- ✓ Use a solicitor and financial advisor who has done a Title Split before
- ✓ There are opportunities everywhere, be relentless on the web
- ✓ You can also contact Global Property Consulting the surveying practice I own.

Example

A 4 story Victorian Terrace was a single unit property when we purchased back in 2010 for an investor, the investor applied for planning permission for 4 flats and completed the flats over the course of 2011. The flats consisted of 2x 1 bedrooms and 2x 2 bedroom; once sold they generated a GDV of around £750,000 and profit of £200,000. The location was ideal for re-sale located within close proximity of Croydon town Centre and original floor plan and four storeys was an ideal layout for conversion.

R- Rent to Rent

It's not new – the concept has been around for a long time, but the name 'Rent to Rent' (or R2R) burst onto the property investment field some years ago, and has been taught as the new way to maximize cash flow. See below the example of one of RENT TO RENT deal.

The idea is simple enough. You source and rent a suitable property and convert it into more lucrative use like Holiday let or HMO (House in Multiple Occupancy.) This 'adds value' to the deal: you rent from the owner/landlord a single let property, and let out each room on an HMO or Holiday let basis, therefore maximizing your rental income.

From the owner's point of view it's ideal: a long term let (five years or more) no voids and no maintenance takes all the pressure off being a landlord. OK, he might have to reduce the rent to the investor, but the offset of no expenses and voids more than makes up for that. There is no real reason to use a letting agency either, unless he wants them to collect the rent for him, so he saves on agency fees.

From the investor's point of view, it can be a way into the property business without having to buy a property.

No problems with finding the deposit for a mortgage, surveys, credit etc. Simply rent a property, convert to an HMO etc., and sit back and watch the cash roll in. However there are few things you need to be careful about. Well, it's not quite as simple it seems. Always consider a couple of things.

First of all, where is the profit in a Rent to Rent deal? It's in the rent you receive for each room in your new HMO. In other words, any HMO will bring you increased rental income (assuming you run it correctly etc.).

You will have to pay a deposit of course, fees for credit rating checks, inventory checks, etc. Then you have to convert the property into an HMO – fire doors, alarms, furniture, possible decoration, white goods, broadband etc. There's other things to consider, too, like will there be enough hot water available when everyone comes home from work and wants a shower. Is one bathroom/shower/toilet enough? Does the cold water storage tank, if applies, have enough capacity for the extra load? whether you need to install a larger one. What about cleaning for the communal area, maintaining the garden, if there is one?

Yes, the start-up costs can be substantial and a big surprise if you're not ready for them. So you need to be prepared for that and plan it properly.

Rent to Rent Example for a house

	Amount
Rent coming in	£2,500
Rent paid to Landlord	£900
All Bills	£400
Maintenance	£120

Total Monthly cash flow	£1,080

Imagine how many R2R deals you need to replace your income.

Remember you would need some funds to set up each property, furnish them and allow some working capital in your bank for contingences. I recommend one should sign a long-term agreement with landlord say 3 to 7 years agreement. Longer the agreement is better for you.

A-Auction purchase

Auctions have always been seen as the place where great deals can be purchased, but how do you maximize your chance of getting one of them?

1. Look for lots being offered by an auction house well outside their area

Especially if they are a regional auctioneer, as they may have a big following in that area, but if they don't you will have less competition bidding on the lot.

2. Look for unusual lots being offered by an auction house

If they are predominately a commercial auctioneer and they have a residential lot (outside their area is even better), they might have less interest in the lot than a residential auctioneer located in the town.

3. Try an offer prior to auction

If you see a property you like the look of, try an offer prior to auction. It will normally have to be at least 'guide price plus', and if accepted you will be need to attend the auctioneer's office to exchange contracts. You will need to be completely comfortable with the legal and physical condition of the property before exchange of contracts and whilst doing this due diligence, the vendor could change their mind for whatever reason. The benefit of buying prior is that if you are successful you would have carried out your due diligence and secured the property at a price that is good for you with the certainty of not being outbid at the auction.

4. Underwriting a lot prior to Auction

Many of the auctioneers will allow you to flip the deal straight away. So you agree a price to purchase prior to action and agree with auctioneer whatever price the property is sold in auction any access will be your profit.

Let me explain this by example.

I agree to buy a property prior to auction at a price of £100,000. I booked my deal by paying 10% to auctioneer and confirmed if property has no bid up to £100,000 then I will buy at £100,000 and pay the remaining 90% funds but if someone buy it for over £100,000 then additional profit is mine. Property was sold for £110,000 in auction room and I made £10,000 without even buying the property. Therefore I effectively made £10,000 profit on my £10,000 which is 100% return in 4 weeks. Isn't it good return, right?

Would you like to learn more strategies like this, we teach many other ways to structuring the deals like this.

5. Register your interest on withdrawn lots

On average about 10% of all lots are withdrawn, this could be because the vendor no longer needs to sell it or the legal documents are not available. Or it was offered vacant and the tenant has not left, or 100s of other reasons. If you see a property you like and noticed it is withdrawn, then ask the auctioneer why and register your interest. It may be that the reason it was withdrawn will be tidied soon, but not before the auction and the auctioneer may well call you when the issue is resolved to offer it to you without the competition of a later auction.

6. Make an offer on unsold lots

Currently 25% of all lots don't sell at auctions. In some cases, these could be considered orphans, with no home to go to. Let's consider the vendors position. He put it to auction so is probably a motivated vendor. He didn't sell it prior, and he could not sell it in the room, so where is he going to go? He will definitely want to have a discussion with you via the auctioneer about you buying it. Try an offer based on the reserve and you can always go up or design your negotiation around their needs to create WIN WIN situation.

T- To Let (buy to Let)

Buy to let is very well known in the market, they are very simple and less hassles deals.

They contain the least risk, you can get lending on them the most easily and they are the easiest to manage. With some cash you can build up a good sized portfolio in a relatively short period of time, predictably increase cash flow per unit, and protect your money from low interest rates and inflation. You can use a local agent to manage the property, so no hassle or not too much of your time involve every month.

E- Exchange with delay completion

Many times you can buy property where you exchange on a property and agree a long completion date. Once you exchange, you basically own it, but you can then 'delay' completion, or own in 'instalments' over a period of time, often many months or years. This could be good when you are buy from motivated seller, family/ relative, waiting for planning, lease extension etc.

This strategy would be also good if you are looking to refurbish or convert the property to get higher mortgage. The value appreciate can be used towards your deposit in many cases, depends how you structure the deal. We teach how to structure this sort of strategies more in details in our workshop.

G- Get control by taking option or lease option

Lease options as name suggest is a contract in which a landlord and tenant agree that, at the end of a specified period, the renter may buy the property. The tenant pays rent plus an additional amount each month. At the end of the lease, the renter may use the cumulative extra payments as a down payment. You can also have just the option rather than lease option if you are not looking to use the place for the agreed period.

This can be the next step from Rent to Rent deal. In rent to rent deal you do not get option to purchase the property. So you are limited to spend your money on the property in R2R. Whereas if you have lease option on the same property you can improve it the way you like and add value that you will get benefit. And you can also sell your lease option deals to someone to encash your profit.

Let me give you an example: I usually tell people, due to my multi skills, that whenever you get stuck with any property related matter just give me a call and I'll find the solution.

One of my contacts gave my details to a lady who was unable to sell her 3 bedroom house for over 6 months in south London. The lady was told that contact Sumit as he is expert and he can find solution for anything.

The lady contacted me and explained me her situation, I met her personally and asked her few question to understand the situation. I asked her what is the price is she looking to achieve? she said around £300,000. And she said but estate agent cannot find any buyer at this price since last 6 months. I asked her how much her mortgage is? She said loan is around £302,000 as she bought the house in 2007 before the market crash. Effectively she had no equity in the house. Even If she would have sold the house for £300,000 (which estate agent could not find any buyer in 6 months) she would have to pay remaining loan and agent fees etc. from her pocket. I asked her what her financial situation is? She said my husband was the only earner in the house who lost job few months ago. And they cannot keep up the mortgage payment. She added if few months more go like this then her house will get repossessed. You can imagine if someone who cannot keep up their mortgage, the condition of their house? yes it was completely run down as they have no funds to maintain the house. No wonder why no one was willing to pay £300,000 for that house in that condition. She is then looking at me with hope as someone said to her that I can find solution for any situation.

I said what if I buy the house for £330,000. She got so excited, I said "we will pay you £330,000 within 18 months' time whenever we are ready but do not worry about your house mortgage payment. We will keep paying your mortgage payment until we complete the transaction by paying £330,000 and you can move on with your life. We then exchange the contract through solicitor by paying £1, yes just £1 and we took over the control of the house on lease option basis with an agreement that we will pay £330,000 within 18 months' time.

What I did thereafter was, I got along with an investor partner and used his funds to completed refurbish the house to the highest standard. Under permitted development I managed to get the 3 meter rear extension of full width of the house added another room into the house and we managed to convert the loft.

So in total we transform this 3 bedroom run down house into 5 bedroom excellent condition house. Within 11 months I found another buyer who was prepare to buy this new 5 bedroom house for £520,000. Yes, completed all conversion and sold within 11 months without even buying the house. All we paid was £1 and cost of refurbishment.

As you would see it was the same house what estate agent could not sell within 6 months. And I had done the deal just in one meeting, created a WIN WIN situation. She got more than what she wanted £330,000 instead of £300,000. I and my investor partner made money without having to buy the house and pay a house down payment etc.

I finally found someone good solicitors who could write a Lease Option contract. It cost me around £1000 plus VAT few years ago. I am still using that contract today, as are my students, but it has changed and been honed massively since that first one. Crucially, I learned how to negotiate with estate agents and owners to get not only the deal, but the best deal.

The good news is that I can teach you the same skills. I run a series of Lease Option Masterclasses through my Property Experts Academy that covers everything you need to know, including the essential negotiation techniques I use. You get all the paperwork and contracts too. If you'd like to know more about Options, any of my other property investing courses or my Personal Mentoring Programme, please visit www.propertyexpertsacademy.com or email me at info@propertyexpertsacademy.com

I-Internal Conversion including commercial conversion

What is Commercial property? Anything that is not residential is commercial like office, warehouse, pub etc.

You may be thinking why do commercial conversion?

Here is the thing, it take same time & hassle but better profit. Would you like 10 BTL OR 2 commercial conversion?

Another reason is Section 24 of the Finance (no. 2) Act 2015 does not apply to commercial property.

Permitted development (prior approval)

✓ Know the rules

- ✓ Know the business better than anyone else
- ✓ It can save you time and money
- ✓ It can help you add massive value
- ✓ It may be remove the need for affordable housing
- ✓ It may remove the Local Authority rights to charge of section 106
- ✓ It will seriously save money and time on planning
- ✓ It may mean you can ignore minimum size requirement
- ✓ It may mean section 24 will not affect your investment
- ✓ It may mean less competition comparatively

I have designed a full 2 days' workshop for this strategy where you learn all about commercial conversion in practical way. Let me explain little bit about how it works.

See below example:

Commercial Conversion Example

	Amount
Bought a Commercial building around 7000 sq. feet	£600,000

	£450,000
Used bank loan @ 5% to get 75% LTV	
Joint venture funds used to purchase	£150,000
Joint venture funds used to convert the building in to 10 flats	£700,000
Sold 10 flats	£2,500,000
Profit made (250000-£600000-£700000-£30,000 interest)	£1,170,000

Profit split with JV partner	£585,000
50:50	

For JV partner making £585,000 extra on his investment of £850000 was great over a period of 12 to 18 months.

E- Extra accommodation for multiple tenants (HMO)

As the name suggest letting the house to multiple tenants. When it comes to HMO's (Houses of Multiple Occupation) they're certainly not all created equal.

Small tweaks in the size, tenant profile and style of your HMO can rapidly increase (or decrease) the cash flowing in to your bank account each and every month.

If you notice in rent to rent example above, the same house that was getting the rent of £900 per month by using HMO strategies one can make more than double rent from the same property using this strategy. This is good strategy to increase the cash floor. But remember HMO is not just an arm chair investment but it's a job unless you have good managing agent who can manage your HMO property at a reasonable fee. That's why I would always recommend an Investor to do HMO deals near their location.

S-Service Accommodation and Holiday let

Service accommodation and Holiday lets are even better cash generating strategy than HMO. The great thing about serviced accommodation as a property investing strategy is that you can do it in houses, bungalows, cottages and apartments. The key is to make the property a home from home as that's what is driving more interest in the sector from holiday makers and professionals looking for short terms stay.

In all of the above strategies you can used one or more joint venture partners to get their money, time and expertise. Just think about if you could use joint ventures for many inputs to do each of these deals, then how many deals can you do like this.

To learn more visit www.propertyexpertsacademy.com

CHAPTER 8: THE BEST INVESTMENT

In my view the best investment is investing time and effort in your own education and personal development.

"The best investment you can make is in yourself"

Warren buffett

The knowledge and skills you gain through educations will stay with you for the rest of your life. Most of the people, the only education they get is the formal education they receive in school, college and university.

Unfortunately, this traditional form of education does not teach you the fundamentals of life about money, investing and creating business.

Since 1999, I have been investing my time and efforts in my own personal development. I am constantly improving myself, my skills and expertise every year and every month. I believe we should never stop leaning. I believe if you stop learning then you will feel as if life is moving slow. I am member of few professional bodies like Royal institute of chartered surveyor (RICS). As part of my professional membership we all need to get our annual CPD, however that's just to keep up to date within the field we are practicing. Likewise, for investing, things are changing so our strategies of investment have to be up to date all the time.

Without appearing to sound arrogant, I have been into real estate for over 17 years and having international property investment experience, yet I do not claim to know all about real estate. I learn something new every day. I am always looking to learn from other successful investors and improve on what I do.

I coached and trained many investors and I've observed that some of the hardest people to teach are the one who have some experience. Sometime, due to their experience they believe they know it all. A little knowledge can be a dangerous thing. Unfortunately, when someone says or thinks "I know this" because they are closing down their mind to new possibilities and opportunity.

Many people are not prepared to put the time, effort or money into educating themselves. I must say, I was very skeptical before I got into personal development. But now, I think spending money to go on to seminar and events are worth because I know if I get just one good idea it will be worth time and money. Each year I commit to spend a certain amount of money and time developing myself further. I really enjoy learning and growing. I understand the value of paying for information and expertise.

I am confident that, if for any reason I were to lose everything today, I would be able to get back to where I am now much quicker, faster and easier than I did the first time because I know exactly what to do this time and maybe more importantly what not to do. How about you? Are you investing enough in yourself? Do you have the skills and knowledge you need to be a successful property investor?

What skills do you need to be a successful investor?

Mental attitude: I firmly believe that you can have all the skills, knowledge and strategies in the world but these are useless if you don't have the right investor's mindset. To be a successful property investor you need to have the right attitude and self-belief that you can achieve anything you put your mind to. Most investors think that investing is all about the strategies and techniques you use. I personally believe that the strategies are 25% and your attitude and mindset are 75% of what it takes to be a really successful property investor.

Positive Outlook: You are generally a positive or a negative person. I know we all go through phases and sometimes we have bad days but I promise you it is easier to achieve what you want if you are positive and looking for the possibilities rather looking for negatives and what can't be done. You get what you think about and focus on. As a property problem solver, you need to be very creative, with the solution-focused outlook. There is always a way. Your role is often to solve problem by finding solution that other people cannot see.

"Make your GOALS so big and inspiring that they make your problems seem insignificant by comparison."

Self-Discipline: To be a successful we something need to push ourselves and do things outside of our comfort zone. It can be very easy to use excuse as to why we have not done something, but really it just comes down to being disciplined and focus on what you want. We may need to make some short- term sacrifice in order to achieve and enjoy long-term benefits.

Having the discipline to do something each day to move you towards your goals will have a massive positive impact on your results.

Numerical skills: Property investing is all about the numbers and return on investment. You need to be able to work out if a deal stacks up or not. Fortunately, you don't have to do this in your head or on the spot, but you do need to understand the numbers upon which you will base your investing decisions. To help people I offer free property deal analyser on my website at www.propertyexpertsacademy.com you can download it for free.

Negotiation skills: As I always maintain throughout this book you need to come up with a solution that is win/win for both you and the seller. You need to be ethical and make sure that you don't take advantage of the sellers' situation. Having said this, the deal has to work for you otherwise there's no point doing it. Remember, this is a business. In most motivated seller purchases there is some scope for negotiation. The level of your negotiation skills can dramatically impact the profitability of your business.

Listening skills: The best way to help a motivated seller is to ask them what they want and listen to what they tell you. As simple as this sound, all too often I hear of investors who talk at motivated sellers rather than talking with them. Building rapport and the trusting relationship is very critical if you want to help these people and secure a good win/win deal. You need to become good at asking question and listening to the answers to make sure you really understand the situation and find the best possible solution for you and the motivated seller.

"Understand the problem of seller and wrap your offer around it"

Research skills: Whenever you find a potential motivated seller lead, you need to act very quickly. Before you move on any deal, you need to quickly assess whether it will work for you. Research is very important. You need to be able to determine the value of a property, the rental potential and realistic rental income that it might achieve. Fortunately, it is extremely easy and quick to do this with the use of the internet these days and the telephone few local agents and experts. You would notice, it can take just 20 to 30 minutes to obtain an estimated valuation that a chartered surveyor would also arrive at using like comparison of similar properties.

Persistence: This is one of the most important skills you can develop. Investing in property is not easy. There are lots of challenges and obstacles you will need to overcome. Your rewards are many times directly linked with these challenges. Unfortunately most people give up for too easily, often just before they achieve the results they are looking for. You need to keep going and remember that if other people have been successful and found a way there is no reason why you can't do the same.

"Fall down 10 times, get up 11th time"

Looking at your current skills set compare to the skills required to be a successful property problem solver, where do you feel that you may need to improve your skills? What can you do to improve your skills?

Remember, you don't have to be good at everything. You can get other people to help you in areas in which you are not so strong. Working with other people is much smarter than doing it on your own, which can be very lonely.

Be smart and Educate yourself smart way

Now that we have recognized the need to constantly improve yourself and develop your skills, knowledge and experience, there are several ways in which you can achieve this. You need to select the methods that best fit with your time and personal requirements. Here are a few ideas for you:

Networking: There are now many very good networking group for property investors in all over the country and world. Attending this event on a regular basis is one of the best ways to develop your knowledge by mixing with and learning from other successful investors. I recognized the incredible value that I had personally gained by learning from and networking with other successful investors. Networking is a low-cost way of gaining knowledge in terms of financial requirements, but it does require some time, effort and dedication from you.

The more investors you know and the bigger your network is, the more opportunities you will become aware of. There are property investors groups all over the UK. I suggest you use the internet to find a group near to where you live or work and start visiting on a regular basis. This is also a great way to keep yourself motivated and on track. Property investing can be lonely sometimes, especially if your friends and family don't really understand what you do. You need to be around like minded people who can give your support, encouragement and advice.

Educational seminar and courses: there are number of individuals and companies in the UK who provide property investment education. Some of them are better than others and it is up to you to decide which is best one for you. Seminars are a great way for you to learn a lot of information very quickly. Although you often have to pay to attend these seminars, the knowledge that you gain will make the investment of time and money very worthwhile. I do offer free seminars many times in the year. Look at my website www.propertyexpertsacademey.com for details or subscribe for such information.

To be honest, given enough time and research, you could probably discover for yourself most of the information that you will learn on a seminar. However the main reason you attend a seminar is to obtain a lot of information, compressed into very short amount of time.

Coaches or mentors: Reading books or attending seminars to learn how to invest in property is pointless unless you put your knowledge into practice. One of the best ways of doing this is to have a coach who will support you, help you to take action and hold you to account. Your coach should be someone who is more experience than you and can add value to investing, help you to grow and expand your knowledge.

My group of companies, provide almost anything that you would need in your property investment journey. If you like to be mentored by us and need any help in your property investment journey, please visit our website and fill up your details with your requirement. I and my team would be more than happy to work with you. I work with motivated and ambitious people just like you that want to quit their 9 to 5 jobs and embrace the

investment route.

Top Tips & Dos & Don'ts

Here are some top tips and some dos and don'ts for investing in property using your money:

1) Invest locally. Get to know your local (highest demand) area and your returns, control and cash flow will increase.

2) Leverage your funds with bank finance to get 500% more cash on cash returns.

3) Buy cheaper properties (middle ground with capital growth) with higher yields (cash flow) and lower risk.

4) Don't go in blind. Get educated, do your research and diligence, do the numbers stack and make financial sense towards your property goals?

5) Create multiple streams of income from different property types such as single-let, multi-let and commercial property conversions.

6) Utilize the many new government tax-saving strategies, such a permised development, commerical to residential conversion and capital allowances etc.

7) Shop around for the best mortgage. Don't just walk to your nearest high street but speak to a reputable independent mortgage broker who will advise and get you the best deals.

8) Know the pitfalls. Have cash buffer for rate rise large maintenance bills or longer than expected void periods.

9) Start now. It's never too late to start but always too late to wait.

ABOUT SUMIT GUPTA

AssocRICS B.Com (Hons) PGDBA (FINANCE) MBA (INTERNATIONAL BUSINESS)

An entrepreneur, Author, Property Investor & Mentor

Sumit Gupta is founder of Property Experts Academy, Global Property Consulting and several other ventures. He has been advising clients and mentoring property investors for over a decade. Sumit Gupta also has helped 100s of people to successfully build their property portfolios.

Sumit Gupta, through his company Global Property Consulting is specialize in advising clients on Investment and disposal, landlord and tenant disputes, lease extension valuation and commercial property rent review, lease renewals, dilapidations and capital allowances claims.

He also acts as Expert witness and Joint Expert witness for various reputed clients in London. He represents clients in tribunal, upper tribunal, court and High court.

Sumit Gupta training programs have been delivered in the UK and India.

Meet Sumit Gupta and receive world-class property investment training at

www.propertyexpertsacademy.com

28212949R00065

Printed in Great Britain
by Amazon